The RUBY

(Short Novel)

The RUBY

(Short Novel)

SELF TRANSLATION OF

KOMBAN COBRA (Malayalam)

SUDHAKARAN K

PREFACE

It were happened to see in a dream

A fierce serpent

Lying on the bottom of a tree

Raised its head, opens mouth and

Look at me.

By mouth widely open,

Raised its head a maximum

It lays an egg in the loose soil,

Crept away and disappeared.

Thus children's novel formed.

Any people alive or dead

And any events past or present

Are not based in this

Children's novel,

Short Novel

DEDICATION

My late father,

Kunhikrishnan Nair,

In holy memory,

CHAPTER – 1

Claramol, She is studying in second class at public school near the city. Her hobby was to spend time every evening when she came home, weeding, watering the plants and enjoying the beauty of the flowers in the garden in front of the house. The garden her mother planted, Claramol managed to look after it when she was in class Lower Kinder Garten, since her mother went to a faraway city for job. She kept making the garden beautiful, surprising mother whenever she came on leave.

Claramol walked to the flower garden as usual one evening. But what greeted her in the garden was a black cobra raising its head and open its mouth. When it saw her, it rose again from earth and stood with its mouth wide open. Claramol was stunned. She could not even scream out loud as if the body were frozen. She stared in horror at the snake's wide open mouth. She wondered if the snake was trying to bite or swallow her.

By the time she gathered all her strength to run away, to her surprise, a white object fell into the soil where she had prepared for planting. The snake curled up and crawled away. Claramol eyed the white object with trepidation and eagerness. It was an egg! A snake egg!

After making sure that the black cobra had passed, she carefully held the egg in her hand. She digs a hole in the moist soil of the garden and lays the egg in it. She frightened if the snake was still in the flower garden. Slowly she walked home. She did not tell her granddad or grandma about the incident. She was afraid that they would take the egg and destroy it.

CHAPTER – 2

The next day after class she walked to the garden as usual. First she checked the place where she had laid the egg the day before. The egg is intact. She took it and placed it in a well sunny place covered with dry grass. Grandma said that the egg hatches due to the warmth of the mother hen which lies above the eggs. Why snake lays egg on the open ground, she wondered. Perhaps the egg laid before it reached the burrow, the young mind found the answer.

She practiced gardening and egg preservation. One evening she came to the garden and saw a baby snake raising its head outside the egg. She jumped with joy.   She hurried inside the house. She took some milk from the milk bottle grandma had kept for the night and went to the garden.

The baby snake was completely exposed by hitting the egg shell and fed it with milk. The baby snake drank the milk and hid among the dry grass.

The next day, Claramol came to the garden with milk, thinking that she would not see the baby snake. But the baby snake heard her footsteps and raised its head. She gave milk to the baby snake like a mother would a baby. Days passed…..

One day the baby snake disappeared when she reaches with milk. She searched the area hoping to see somewhere nearby, but was disappointed. Saddened, she reached the threshold, unable to concentrate on reading, Claramol was sad.

In the following days, she reached the garden eager to see the baby snake, but the result was disappointment. The days have passed. Claramol's flower garden is growing beautiful with flowers of various colours. Everyone who saw Claramol was sincerely praised. She held her head high proudly. She became a star among her classmates and teachers.

CHAPTER – 3

One day after a few weeks she was strolling through the flower garden. It was then that she noticed the dry leaves lying on the ground moving. She bent down and stared at the floor. A small black snake crawls among the dry leaves.

The snake raised its head and looked at her. She cut a piece of the boiled egg she was eating and put it on a leaf and stood back a little. The snake slowly crawled up and ate the egg, unfolding the curled up form again. After a while the snake crawled back and disappeared through a stone crevice. That's when Claramol caught her breath.

'A snake bites the hand that gave milk,' she had heard auntie often say about many people.

Will the snake bite me?

Claramol remembered how neighbour Mridula's mother was bitten by a cobra while harvesting paddy in the field of us and she died. She also remembered going with her mother to see their dead body. She remembered with horror their corpse lying stretched out in the blue. She hurriedly walked to the threshold.

CHAPTER – 4

The chickens, cows and calves in this house all have different name, she thought when she reached the bedroom. Call that name and they will approach fast. It is usual. She took out a piece of paper and thought about naming her baby snake, which should have been done a little earlier, as the snake grew bigger. Cobra is the English name of this type of snake. She thought deeply. With a smug note she wrote on the paper,

'Komban, Komban Cobra.'

The next day she came to the garden and called out in a loud voice,

"Komba….. Komba……"

Calling its name loudly, she walked here and there everywhere through the garden. Her baby snake was nowhere to be seen. Her eyes fell on a newly blooming rose in the garden.

A rose bush is full of blooming roses. They are gently swaying in the wind. After taking a selfy, she started taking selfies in various poses in front of the rose plant. When mother bought the new mobile phone, the old one was given to her to use at home. It's time to light the lamp in the veranda.

She turned back to veranda. When she reached veranda, she kept sending the photos she had taken one by one to her father, mother and classmates. After sending them to everyone, she looked at each photo again one by one. In the final photo, Komban Cobra is perched by raising its head over rose petals, above her head.

How to save the Komban Cobra? She thought and thought. Granddad's and grandma's mobile phones started ringing continuously. On the other side are father, mother, relatives and classmates. She realized that the topic of conversation was about seeing a snake in the selfy. Granddad and grandma called the neighbours. They prepared for a detailed inspection in the garden.

Short Novel

Claramol deliberately pretends fear of snake, did not bother to go to the flower garden. If she goes, the Komban Cobra will come down from the hole. Maybe they'll all just beat it or get caught and deported by the Forest department, she remembered with pain. She checked the selfy again and again. Behind her stands Komban Cobra raising its head and perched high above the rose petals. A few hours later, a group of about 10 people returned in desperation with sticks, emergencies and torches. They could not even see the dust of the snake. Claramol laughed inside. She remembered. 'The Komban Cobra is clever, very clever.'

CHAPTER – 5

Later, Claramol were banned from going to the garden.

"Do not go into the garden alone." Granddad said.

That was also the stand of the other parents. However, she kept throwing half of the eggs that were given to her into the garden without anyone noticing.

One day Claramol became stubborn,

"I want to go to the garden"

"There will be a snake, it is a black cobra, we will not agree to go", said the granddad.

"Then granddad go and look, if there is no snake, let me go"

At last the granddad examined the garden in detail, the inside and outside of the garden were cleaned and Claramol were allowed to go. She jumped with joy. She began to walk through the garden, caressing the flowers and calling loudly 'Komba….., Komba…...' She went to the stone gap where the Komban Cobra had gone and looked carefully.

"Komba….." she called loudly once more.

The cobra shows its head and neck out of the gap in the stone and raised its head in front of her. After eating the egg she gave to it, Komban Cobra disappeared into the V-Tow of the stone. Claramol came to the room and immersed herself in her studies. Now she can study with enthusiasm. She couldn't contain her joy.

CHAPTER – 6

Sometimes Komban Cobra is not seen for days and sometimes for weeks. But she didn't change her routine. Komban Cobra, like me would have to go to school and prepare the garden, or be busy finding food, and the daily absences would be due to the rush, she consoled herself.

Mine is a house surrounded by stone walls with a huge iron gate in front. The wall is built in this way to avoid the harm of wild animals such as dogs, pigs and foxes. Therefore, I could walk around the field without fear of anything, and I used to walk around like that.

CHAPTER – 7

It was a Thursday. The school was closed that day due to the death of a minister of state. I was walking through the yard stalking after the butterflies to catch them. Suddenly a car is seen stopping in front of the gate of the house. A white beautiful auntie wearing a red sari and black sunglass got out of it and slowly opened the gate.

The knowledge of the gang of child abductors flashed through my mind as I passed out for a moment after seeing their masquerades. I turned around and tried to run inside but the auntie caught me and filled my mouth with a scarf and held me tightly and tried to walk with me towards the car.

I cried out loudly saying 'Oop' but no one could hear my voice because auntie filled my mouth with a scarf. The woman grabbed me and walked towards the car. Suddenly, She screamed "Oop" and ran towards the car.

When I look, Komban raised its head and standing beside me. By the time the granddad, grandma and uncle who were at home came running after hearing the commotion, the woman had run towards the car and fell down. Two men in the car quickly took her into the car and drove away.

Uncle followed the car on his motor bike. Granddad and grandma took care. I explained, the woman filled my mouth with a scarf, I bite her hand, and seeing my granddad and others coming, she ran away from me, approached the car and fell by hitting on a stone. I searched for the Komban Cobra. Komban Cobra was nowhere to be seen.

By that time uncle returned. There was no number plate behind the car! And the car can't follow which droves at high speed through the traffic without caring any traffic signals!

Short Novel

"No matter, I informed the police, they will do everything, they will not miss a trace", uncle said.

Short Novel

CHAPTER – 8

The new Head Master took Charge. He is a distant relative of school Manager! A man who was black and fat, hairy all over his body, larger in size rather than normal human beings. He instilled fear in children just by looking at him. The head master said in the school assembly.

"Next year our pass percentage should be hundred and we should excel in extra-curricular activities and sports events at the district level. Each child needs to be monitored individually."

From the next day every child was required to come to the Head Master's room after leaving school in the evening.

The information about the parents of students, the learning style of the children at home and the quality of the children's learning all are checked by the head master.

One day, two men were walking along the road in front of the school with an elephant.

The bell tied around the elephant's neck was making noise nnim….. nnim…..

All our classmates ran to the classroom window and watched the elephant in full. That's when the head master who was strolling through the veranda with a cane reached the classroom. The head master came to the classroom and called Neeraj beside him. "Where do you care? Hold out your hand?" The head master's cane rose several times in Neerji's outstretched hand.

The class teacher and all my classmates also left. We all came to the window to see the elephant. But I thought the head master must have seen only Neeraj.

I understood the truth when my friends told me. Neeraj was called to the head master's office room yesterday evening! Along with questioning the children, the head master's hands are caressing the body parts of the children.

The head master usually harasses those who show non-co-operation.

When the head master touches Neeraj's body,

"Don't touch my body" said Neeraj.

As revenge the headmaster beats him on a favourable circumstance.

The children were afraid to tell the Head Master's actions at home.

If anyone did, they will have to receive punishment from the head master. Moreover, if children gave information to the parents sometimes they are not allowed to go to school.

CHAPTER – 9

Days passed. One day the school peon handed over a list to the class teacher. Claramol was overwhelmed. She is to meet the Head Master tomorrow evening. Claramol was worried. After the classes over she went home and spent a long time in the garden.

She looked for the Komban Cobra in the garden, but in vain.

"Komba….., I have to go to the head master's room tomorrow. Will that scoundrel harm me?" She was saying it at the top of her voice.

Granddad and grandma are watching TV inside the house. They have poor hearing and the TV is on at maximum volume. Therefore, Claramol was sure that they would not hear her loud voice from the garden.

But Komban Cobra was not seen anywhere in the area. Suppressing her grief, she walked into the house. Many times in her sleep she woke up with nightmare. It was dawn. She thought about not going to school today. At last, come what may, she decided to go to school.

She started stuffing the books in her school bag as per the timetable. Claramol opened the side cover of the bag and was amazed. Komban Cobra is sound asleep on the side cover. She carefully shouldered her bag and walked to the school bus stop.

When she reached the school, she took the required books and kept the bag safely in the corner of the classroom. During the interval she took her bag to change the book. The Komban Cobra is missing from the bag. She checked the bag several times. No, the Komban Cobra is out of the bag. She worried if the Komban Cobra would leave her.

It was evening. The bell rang. The classmates started walking towards the school bus. Claramol hesitated and went to the head master's room.

"Honey…" The Head Master who was sitting on the chair called out to her, putting a hand on her shoulder and trying to keep her close.

"Oop….." Claramol cried unknowingly.

"Oop….., snakebites me…..   " shouted the Head Master even more loudly.

The teachers and students who had boarded the school bus rushed to the head master's room after hearing the screams of the head master.

The Head Master was in a semi-conscious state, bleeding from his lower leg. The other teachers looked for the snake but found nothing in the area. Claramol ran to the classroom and took her bag. The Komban Cobra itself lies in anticipation. She picked up her bag and walked towards the school bus vigorously.

She left the Komban Cobra in the garden after making sure free of porches and that no one noticed.

"Thanks…, Komba…, a thousand thanks …!"

Komban Cobra raised its head and looked at her putting its tongue outside. She happily walked into the house.

CHAPTER – 10

It was Bharat band then. It was half past eleven in the morning and the rustling of dry leaves in the parcel of land outside the yard was unusual. I was curious about something. I looked out into the yard.

Komban Cobra and a big mongoose were fighting each other in the dry leaves where the dry leaves piled up. They are in a life and death struggle. I felt stunned. If snake and mongoose fight themselves, mongoose will win in the end. Mongoose will bite the snake and kill it. It is the knowledge that I got from my granddad.

There is no time to think. She rushed to the field were fighting took place. A big stone was thrown aiming mongoose's head. Luckily, stone hit the mongoose's head sharply and it rolled over three times and lay motionless. Instantly, Komban Cobra bite mongoose and threw it away in the sky.

Mongoose fell to the ground and ran into a burrow with death threats. I went near to the Komban Cobra. Claramol was sure something had happened to the Komban Cobra in the fight. She ran to the kitchen, came back with a handful of turmeric powder and sprinkled it all over the Komban Cobra's body, the medicine

Short Novel

the mother did when the chick was saved after hawking last week.

Will it work or not? She looked at the Komban Cobra, it shortened the form and crawled through the turmeric powder that fell on the ground and smeared its body with turmeric powder and crawled to her feet.

Chapter – 11

It was a Sunday. The granddad who went to the market returned and showed her a white small bottle and asked,

"Do you know Claramol, what's in this bottle?", granddad asked.

"How can I know without exposing the bottle?", I asked back.

Granddad opened the bottle and said,

"This is asafoetida, the milk asafoetida, where the smell of this reaches, no snake will come. Just mix it with water and spray it to drive away snakes nearby."

Claramol smelled danger. She took the bottle from her granddad's hand and smelled it. Suddenly she started sneezing. "Oh, it's a headache," she cried, clutching her head.

The granddad became gloomy. "What man, what have you bought and brought to kill the baby?", grandma was angry towards granddad. "Never mind, dear, granddad may just return it to the shop where I bought it."

Granddad immediately left for the market. Lucky no one understood my formula. She chuckled on the bed with heart full joy.

CHAPTER – 12

One day Komban Cobra and I were playing in the garden after dinner. An English movie song that I had knew and by heart was being sung loudly. The Komban Cobra was blown and swayed to the song.

Suddenly there was a sound like something crawling. The form was shortened and the Komban rushed to out of the garden like a bolt of lightning. A full snake more than twice its size with spots all over its body ran after Komban Cobra for catching. Claramol was overwhelmed by this. Claramol don't know what to do.

Hesitating she ran after the big snake which is running after Komban Cobra. Komban Cobra was scrambling for its life, twisting, turning and flipping in front of the running snake as if Komban Cobra had not been touched. The moment the snake seemed to have put the Komban Cobra in its mouth, the big snake was moving backwards as if someone had grabbed it by the tail and pulled it.

Claramol was stunned. A huge snake is devouring the snake that ran behind the Komban Cobra. After swallowing the snake whole, it raised its head and looked at Claramol. After that the form shrank and crawled away.

Claramol was surprised. It is Komban Cobra's mother? A mother who saved her child in time!

She searched Komban Cobra nearby. Komban Cobra is watching everything from a tree branch. Tired of running, she gave a 'Tata' to the Komban and walked inside of the house.

CHAPTER – 13

After the interval, the bell rang in the school. All the children entered their classrooms. In Claramol's class, Maths teacher Swarna began to explain how to find LCM of fractions.

Claramol felt her head spins. Suddenly she fell to the floor with her head spinning. The teachers and classmates took her to the hospital. After detailed examination by expert doctors found a deadly virus is multiplying all over in her body.

Doctors were searching the Internet for an antidote to the virus. The result was only disappointment, even after talking to expert doctors abroad, they also did not know about the antidote against the said virus.

By that time, her granddad and grandma had reached the hospital. In front of everyone, doctors said,

"This disease is affected very early. It is now that the virus has gained the upper hand to break down the immune system. She's almost sinking. A miracle must happen if she is to be saved." Doctors knew that concealing the truth was not in line with medical ethics.

A snake crawled towards the door of the ICU scaring everyone. People including doctors were scattered all around. The security man opened the door of the ICU to escape and when he tried to escape, the snake also entered the ICU.

Nurses and other staff rushed out of the ICU after seeing security man running and the snake crawling. Eagerly, everyone looked through the glass of the ICU.

The snake crawled to the bed of Claramol. The snake carefully looked at the face of the unconscious Claramol. Then spread the foam and forcefully blow three times into the nose of the Claramol. Claramol slowly opened her eyes. Seeing Komban Cobra, Claramol got up, forgot the surroundings and called 'Komba....' and hugged the Komban Cobra.

By the time granddad, grandma, doctors and other medical workers came near to Clara mol, Komban Cobra moved under the coat.

The doctors took turns examining her. After examining her blood sample, they realized that all the viruses that caused the disease in her body were destroyed. She is healthy.

Psychiatric doctor Nainika counselled her.

'Any previous connection with the snake is the question?'

"Yes, of course. This same snake was seen above her head in Claramol's selfy", the granddad testified.

Short Novel

Claramol could not hide anything from the doctor. She opened up about what happened since she got the snake egg till now.

"Great, a rare medicine to cure a rare disease," doctor sincerely appreciated Claramol.

"Doctor, what should we do with the snake?" Everyone asked.

"You don't have to do anything, but let it go safely."

Everyone searched for the snake under the bed, under the coat and all over the ICU.

But not even the dust of the snake was visible. Later that was the only topic of conversation there,

'The friend Komban Cobra saved the life of Claramol!'

CHAPTER – 14

Even though Claramol returned home, the media did not leave. They want to see the Komban Cobra.

The doctors said that, 'She needs complete rest now', but the media people were not ready to go away.

"I will call when the Komban Cobra comes, just give your mobile number", Claramol said.

But by that time, a section of the media prepared scoops and broadcasted that it was a lie that Komban Cobra saved the life of Clara mol.

After two days, cheerful Claramol went to the garden and called out loudly,

"Komba...... , Komba......"

Komban Cobra came out of a nearby pot. She fed Komban Cobra with pre-stored food items including chicken eggs.

Then she took hold of the Komban Cobra and began to wrap it around her left hand. She called all the media people, the message was,
'I am ready to show Komban Cobra, come soon'.

Suspicious, Komban hurried away from her. Claramol did not leave. She held Komban tightly. After some time media vehicles started rushing towards the compound of her house.

She welcomed the Media's, clutching the Komban Cobra in her left hand. She answered the media's questions by holding the Komban Cobra close to her body and caressing the form. At first it tried to evade, but slowly Komban Cobra rose to the occasion.

At last it rose up on its own tail and stood tall next to Claramol 's head. By resting its head on the shoulder of Claramol, raising its form and putting its tongue out it rocks and rocks.

At last the form shrank down and quickly disappeared through the dry leaves. Happy for getting a viral incident, the Media's left by giving Claramol a handful of gifts.

From the next day her house was crowded with visitors. Since it was Christmas vacation, it did not affect her studies. But she did not bother to show Komban Cobra to the visitors.

Her reasoning was that she had no idea where Komban Cobra was now. One day she fell asleep after having lunch. Suddenly, her attention was drawn by the chatter from outside.

"One crore! If you show us Komban Cobra and allow us to catch it, we will give you rupees one crore in cash."

Claramol looked out through the keyhole in the door.

A red beard man and a fat white man. From their conversation, she was understood that the one who was talking was a scientist and the other with him was the MLA of the locality.

"Okay", said the granddad, "I need time, I will call when I see the Komban Cobra."

"Okay, please take some time. But don't be put off. Let this be in hand", they put a bundle of notes in the granddad's hand, said 'Good bye' and left.

Claramol turned and tossed in bed. She didn't know what to do.

Short Novel

"Honey….., Claramol…..", granddad came into the room to wake me up.

"Get out", Claramol can't contain her rage.

"I say you get out," she ordered.

She saw her granddad looking gloomy and sweating.

Grandma heard the commotion and came running there.

"Was the Komban Cobra sold for one crore rupees with the grandma's knowledge?" She raised her voice to her grandma.

"Sold the Komban Cobra? who to whom? when? Grandma asked.

Short Novel

She took ten bundles of five hundred rupees notes from the table and threw them on the floor.

"Look, advance of the contract to sell the Komban Cobra," she called out.

"What man, this snake that saved our baby's life. Sell it, it won't happen here."

Please return advance soon, grandma gave support to Claramol. The granddad, who was pale and pale, immediately said that he should buy back the advance on the mobile phone and that he would not give the Komban Cobra. I know the character of granddad. He is a poor man, perfect and lovely. It was a decision taken under pressure and excess

Short Novel

of money, thinking that no one would know. I shouldn't have shouted. But, there was no other way to save the Komban Cobra, she tried to comfort herself.

CHAPTER - 15

The next evening, a Chevrolet car stopped in front of the gate of the house. Out of that, a bearded man in red and a man with a shaved head, who gave admittance to my granddad yesterday, came towards our house.

Granddad took them in and explained the matter in detail.

"Is this your final decision? Is there no change?" asked the man in red.

"No," said the granddad.

"Then you will be sad. The snake is taken for expensive experiments. We will take the Komban Cobra at any cost." He threatened.

"Sir, please don't hurt our daughter." Granddad was humbled.

"We don't care about the suffering of one child if it benefits thousands of children."

The Scientist took back the advance and left the place.

He is a world famous doctor and scientist. He just won't say anything. Granddad bowed his head in sorrow. Claramol did not get any grip after that thought.

Anyway, just give the Komban Cobra a warning. She stomped hard on the floor of the garden. It was a warning to Komban Cobra for danger. The Komban

Cobra raised its head out of the hole and pulled its tongue out three times.

She knew that Komban Cobra understood threatens. The Komban Cobra did not come out after that.

Short Novel

CHAPTER – 16

The next morning at around 10 o'clock, two huge vans stopped in front of the gate of the house. Out of one came the scientist, local village officer and a drug expert, Officials of Forest department from the other. They were also preparing to check inside the house if needed. They showed her granddad the order to capture the Komban Cobra for public medical experiments.

"Sir, ... " But granddad couldn't utter anything.

"Where is your friend Komban Cobra?" Scientist asked Claramol

"It was nowhere to be seen. It will be seen here anywhere", the memory of child actor in English cinema made her brave.

"Search" ordered the scientist.

They searched the house, inside, outside and premises.

"Sir, a uropelties ceylanica", joked a forest official looking at a blind-snake on the premise.

"Won bumper prize," joked another official with a laugh.

"Be serious, do your duty", warned superior officer.

They checked again and again everywhere inside, outside the house and in the premises, but they could not find a single dust of Komban Cobra. They were disappointed and about to go back.

We will come again, he can't hide all the time" said the scientist looking at her granddad and walking towards the vehicle.

The scientist got into the vehicle, "Oop, I've been bitten by a snake", screamed loudly.

In no time Kompan Cobra got out of the vehicle and crawled through the dry leaves silently towards the garden unnoticed. Officers searched the vehicle but did not find the snake. As soon as they lost their balance, they drove towards hospital.

"Clever! Komban Cobra is very clever!. He bitten the scientist himself" the locals couldn't stop laughing.

Days and weeks passed. No movement is seen on the part of the scientists or officials. Maybe they were waiting for the scientist to recover, thought Clara mol.

In any case, she kept giving warnings to Komban Cobra. Sometimes Komban Cobra went missing for weeks. She thought to herself that the Komban Cobra was in some sort of preparation.

CHAPTER -17

One day Claramol woke up after hearing the roar of a vehicle. In front of the gate is the huge car of the scientist, followed by the police and forest vehicles. Three dogs in a vehicle in the back, followed by an ambulance in full set up.

Claramol shivered.

'Oh! God! How I will save Komban Cobra', she thought.

Those who came in the vehicle released the dogs to the courtyard without saying anything to anyone. These are dogs specially trained to detect snakes.

The dogs were barking inside and around the house. Meanwhile, they were looking up at the sky and barking. The narcotics experts were in a dilemma. What happens to the dogs?

Instead of tracing the snake, it runs and barks in all directions. Officers bathed in sweat. After some time the barking of the dogs stopped. The dog trainer who went to search for the dogs saw only the lifeless carcasses of the dogs.

On getting the information, the commando got out of the police jeep with a stun gun and moved towards the house from the gate. For a moment, a python fell from the upper branch of a mango tree onto commando's body and started circling around commando, including the Stun gun.

The Stun gun, which was prepared at full load, started firing continuously. Fortunately, the bullets did not hit the house. The convoy, which was parked on the roadside, started to burst into flames, including ambulance.

By the time the dutiful police and narcotics expert opportunistically rushed at the python with guns, a bunch of baby snakes had crawled into their pants. Some of the officers fell unconscious after being bitten by the small snakes. Conscious people ran screaming down the road. A huge black cobra ran towards the scientist who was standing dumbfounded by the gate. It began to haunt the scientist. With a roar, the scientist fell flat on the ground. Claramol realized that the snake was Komban Cobra's mother.

The Komban Cobra ran towards a senior police Inspector standing in the middle of the road. The police inspector took Claramol's photo from his pocket and held it with both hands in front of his body. Komban Cobra was looking carefully at the photo by standing its tail. The inspector was walking back slowly, very slowly. The inspector, when reached at a safe distance, noticed the Komban Cobra. The Komban Cobra had shortened the form and crawled back. The inspector gave a kiss to the photo of Claramol and put it in the pocket.

Then he turned on the wireless set and he called the headquarters control room.

"King Mongoose Speaking, Operation Komban Cobra Over. The Komban Cobra could not be captured alive. Our men also have serious injuries. Send two ambulances and a police jeep immediately, over."

Within fifteen minutes, the police jeep and the ambulances rushed there.

They carefully examined the scientist lying on the ground. A long time has passed since he left this world. The inspector took the hat and gave respect to the corpse.

Meanwhile, the locals had caught a small snake. Examination revealed that the small snakes belonged to the non-venomous class of water snakes.

"Where is the Komban cobra's carcass?" Superior Officer who came there asked to the Inspector.

"Sorry sir, I lost my attention for a moment and got carried away by the hawk."

The superior Officer looked at the inspector carefully.

The inspector looked up at the sky to see if there was any hawk there. Inspector had only the same way to protect Komban Cobra and Claramol.

Short Novel

CHAPTER – 18

The seasons spring, summer, autumn and winter were changed year by year. Clara mol's garden was also shining with its ancient beauty. Claramol too had become a full grown woman.

Like any young woman, it was a dream come true day for Claramol. It was her wedding day, her auspicious day.

Under the supervision of the beautician, her friends were dressing her up with ornaments and making her look very beautiful. But as one would expect, her eyes were darting around.

Relatives, friends and neighbours are chatting inside the house, outside and in the yard.

Suddenly there was a divine light. A huge snake crawled into the yard after raising its head and biting something in its mouth. Those who gathered there made way for the snake to go with fear and respect. The murmur of 'Komban Cobra' was echoing in the air.

Slowly the snake climbed up the veranda and crawled into Claramol's room. Seeing the Komban Cobra at the door, Clara mol happily welcomed "Komba......, Komba......" and hugged the Komban cobra.

Komban Cobra gave the ruby he had brought to Claramol as a wedding gift. After eating the eggs and milk given by Claramol, He raised its head and put tongue outside and moved the tongue three times and wished for good luck for marriage.

On his way back to the garden, he did not forget to go in front of the inspector, one of the guests present, and express his gratitude.

"Sir, You have reported that the Komban Cobra was killed and the hawk took away its carcass," asked a local resident.

"That's right, now it may another snake which was in the group that day." The

Short Novel

inspector once again kept the good secret he had concealed and provided complete safety to Claramol and Komban Cobra.